U0111781

大展好書　好書大展
品嘗好書　冠群可期

大展好書　好書大展
品嘗好書　冠群可期

▲作者的少林拳　Shaolin Boxing of the Author

▲武術雜誌上的耿軍
Geng Jun on the Cover of Wushu Magazine

▲英法武術代表團訪問孟州少林武術院
The Wushu Delegation of France and UK is visiting the Meng zhou Shaolin Wushu Institute

▲作者部分弟子參加武打片拍攝
Parts of students of author take part in fliming Acrobatic fighting film

▲作者與恩師素法大師
The Author and his Teacher Grandmaster Sufa

▲作者指導女兒耿瑞濤練功
The Author is coaching his daughter to practise her skill

▲作者與原國家武術協會主席張耀庭
The Author and the former Chairman of the Chinese Wushu
Association Zhang Yaoting

▲作者的少林拳　Shaolin Boxing of the Author

▲武術雜誌封面上的耿軍
Geng Jun on the Cover of Wushu Magazine

▲作者與恩師素法大師
The Author and his Teacher Grandmaster Sufa

▲作者率領國外弟子朝拜少林寺　Author leads foreign students to visit Shaolin Temple

▲作者與武僧教頭德揚師兄在捶譜堂
In Chuipu Hall, the author and his senior fellow apprentice
who is also the wushu monk teacher deyang

▲作者與中國政協副主席萬國權
The Author and the vice Chairman of the Chinese People's Political
Consultative Conference （CPPCC）Wan Guoquan

▲作者傳藝國際黑帶功夫總會
The Author is teaching his Wushu skill in International
Black Belt Kungfu Federation

▲作者指導兒子耿鵬飛練功
The Author is coaching his son Geng Pengfei to practise
his skill

少林傳統功夫漢英對照系列　❶

Shaolin Traditional Kungfu Series Books　❶

七星螳螂拳

Seven-star Mantis Boxing（White-Ape Offering Book）

白猿獻書

耿軍　著

Written by Geng Jun

大展出版社有限公司

作者簡介

　　耿軍（法號釋德君），1968 年 11 月出生於河南省孟州市，係少林寺三十一世皈依弟子。中國武術七段、全國十佳武術教練員、中國少林武術研究會副秘書長、焦作市政協十屆常委、濟南軍區特警部隊特邀武功總教練、洛陽師範學院客座教授、英才教育集團董事長。1989 年創辦孟州少林武術院、2001 年創辦英才雙語學校。先後獲得河南省優秀青年新聞人物、全國優秀武術教育家等榮譽稱號。

　　1983 年拜在少林寺住持素喜法師和著名武僧素法大師門下學藝，成爲大師的關門弟子，後經素法大師引薦，又隨螳螂拳一代宗師李占元、金剛力功于憲華等大師學藝。在中國鄭州國際少林武術節、全國武林精英大賽、全國武術演武大會等比賽中 6 次獲得少林武術冠軍；在中華傳統武術精粹大賽中獲得了象徵少林武術最高榮譽的「達摩杯」一座。他主講示範的 36 集《少林傳統功夫》教學片已由人民體育音像出版社出版發行。他曾多次率團出訪海外，在國際武術界享有較高聲譽。

　　他創辦的孟州少林武術院，現已發展成爲豫北地區最大的以學習文化爲主、以武術爲辦學特色的封閉式、寄宿制學校，是中國十大武術教育基地之一。

Brief Introduction to the Author   作者簡介

Geng Jun（also named Shidejun in Buddhism）, born in Mengzhou City of Henan Province, November 1968, is a Bud-dhist disciple of the 31st generation, the 7th section of Chinese Wu shu, national "Shijia" Wu shu coach, Vice Secretary General of China Shaolin Wu shu Research Society, standing committee member of 10th Political Consultative Conference of Jiaozuo City, invited General Kungfu Coach of special police of Jinan Military District, visiting professor of Luoyang Normal University, and Board Chairman of Yingcai Education Group. In 1989, he estab-lished Mengzhou Shaolin Wu shu Institute; in 2001, he estab-lished Yingcai Bilingual School · He has been successively awarded honorable titles of "Excellent Youth News Celebrity of Henan Province" "State Excellent Wu shu Educationalist" etc.

In 1983, he learned Wu shu from Suxi Rabbi, the Abbot of Shaolin Temple, and Grandmaster Sufa, a famous Wu shu monk, and became the last disciple of the

Grandmaster. Then recom-mended by Grandmaster Sufa, he learned Wu shu from masters such as Li Zhanyuan, great master of mantis boxing, and Yu Xianhua who specializes in Jingangli gong. He won the Shaolin Wu shu champion for 6 times in China Zhengzhou International Wu shu Festival, National Competition of Wu lin Elites, National Wu shu Performance Conference, etc. and one "Damo Trophy" that symbolizes the highest honor of Shaolin Wu shu in Chinese Traditional Wu shu Succinct Competition. 36 volumes teaching VCD of Shaolin Traditional Wu shu has been published and is-sued by People's Sports Audio Visual Publishing House. He has led delegations to visit overseas for many times, enjoying high reputation in the martial art circle of the world.

Mengzhou Shaolin Wu shu Institute, established by him, has developed into the largest enclosed type boarding school of Yubei (north of Henan Province) area, which takes knowledge as primary and Wu shu as distinctiveness, also one of China's top ten Wu shu education bases.

序　言

　　中華武術源遠流長，門類繁多。

　　少林武術源自嵩山少林寺，因寺齊名，是我國拳系中著名的流派之一。少林寺自北魏太和十九年建寺以來，已有一千五百多年的歷史。而少林武術也決不是哪一人哪一僧所獨創，它是歷代僧俗歷經漫長的生活歷程，根據生活所需逐步豐富完善而成。

　　據少林寺志記載許多少林僧人在出家之前就精通武術或慕少林之名而來或迫於生計或看破紅塵等諸多原因削髮爲僧投奔少林，少林寺歷來倡武，並經常派武僧下山，雲遊四方尋師學藝。還請武林高手到寺，如宋朝的福居禪師曾邀集十八家武林名家到寺切磋技藝，推動了少林武術的發展，使少林武術得諸家之長。

　　本書作者自幼習武，師承素喜、素法和螳螂拳李占元等多位名家，當年如饑似渴在少林寺研習功夫，曾多次在國內外大賽中獲獎。創辦的孟州少林武術院亦是全國著名的武術院校之一，他示範主講的 36 集《少林傳統功夫》教學 VCD 已由人民體育音像出版社發行。

　　本套叢書的三十多個少林傳統套路和實戰技法是少

林武術的主要內容，部分還是作者獨到心得，很值得一讀，該書還採用漢英文對照，使外國愛好者無語言障礙，爲少林武術走向世界做出了自己的貢獻，亦是可喜可賀之事。

　　　　　　　　　　　　　　張耀庭題
　　　　　　　　　　　　　　甲申秋月

Preface

序
言

Chinese Wushu is originated from ancient time and has a long history, it has various styles.

Shaolin Wushu named from the Shaolin Temple of Songshan Mountain, it is one of the famous styles in the Chinese boxing genre. Shaolin temple has more than 1500 years of history since its establishment in the 19th year of North Wei Taihe Dynasty. No one genre of Shaolin Wushu is created solely by any person or monk, but completed gradually by Buddhist monks and common people from generation to generation through long–lasting living course according to the requirements of life. As recording of Record of Shaolin Temple, many Shaolin Buddhist monks had already got a mastery of Wushu before they became a Buddhist monk, they came to Shaolin for tonsure to be a Buddhist monk due to many reasons such as admiring for the name of Shaolin, or by force of life or seeing through thevanity of life. The Shaolin Temple always promotes Wushu and frequently appoints Wushu Buddhist monks to go down the mountain to roam around for searching masters and learning Wushu from them. It also invites

七星螳螂拳白猿献书

Wushu experts to come to the temple, such as Buddhist monk Fuju of Song Dynasty, it once invited Wushu famous exports of 18 schools to come to the temple to make skill interchange, which promoted the development of Shaolin Wushu and made it absorb advantages of all other schools.

The author learned from many famous exports such as Suxi, Sufa and Li Zhanyuan of Mantis Boxing, he studied Chinese boxing eagerly in Shaolin Temple, and got lots of awards both at home and abroad, he also set up the Mengzhou Shaolin Wushu Institute, which is one of the most famous Wushu institutes around China. He makes demonstration and teaching in the 36 volumes teaching VCD of Shaolin Traditional Wushu, which have been published by Peoples sports Audio Visual publishing house.

There are more than 30 traditional Shaolin routines and practical techniques in this series of books, which are the main content of Shaolin Wushu, and part of which is the original things learned by the author, it is worthy of reading. The series books adopt Chinese and English versions, make foreign fans have no language barrier, and make contribution to Shaolin Wushu going to the world, which is delighting and congratulating thing.

Titled by Zhang Yaoting

目　錄
Contents

七星螳螂拳白猿獻書

說　明

　　（一）為了表述清楚，以圖像和文字對動作作了分解說明，練習時應力求連貫銜接。

　　（二）在文字說明中，除特別說明外，不論先寫或後寫身體的某一部分，各運動部位都要求協調活動、連貫銜接，切勿先後割裂。

　　（三）動作方向轉變以人體為準，標明前後左右。

　　（四）圖上的線條是表明這一動作到下一動作經過的線路及部位。左手、左腳及左轉均為虛線（┈┈►）；右手、右腳及右轉均為實線（──►）。

Instructions

(i) In order to explain clearly figures and words are used to describe the actions in multi steps. Try to keep coherent when exercising.

(ii) In the word instruction, unless special instruction, each action part of the body shall act harmoniously and join coherently no matter it is written first or last, please do not separate the actions.

(iii) The action direction shall be turned taking body as standard, which is marked with front, back, left or right.

(iv) The line in the figure shows the route and position from this action to the next action. The left hand, left foot and turn left are all showed in broken line (------►) ; the right hand, right foot and turn right are all showed in real line (——►) .

基本步型與基本手型
Basic stances and Basic hand forms

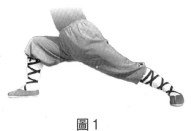

圖 1

圖 2

圖 3

圖 4

圖 5

圖 6

圖 7

圖 8

圖 9

圖 10

圖 11

圖 12

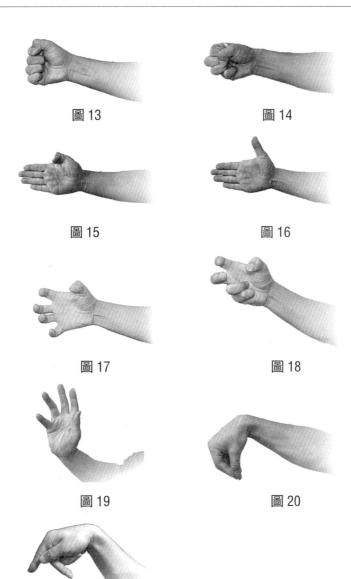

圖 13

圖 14

圖 15

圖 16

圖 17

圖 18

圖 19

圖 20

圖 21

基本步型與基本手型

基本步型

　　少林武術中常見的步型有：弓步、馬步、仆步、虛步、歇步、坐盤步、丁步、併步、七星步、跪步、高虛步、翹腳步 12 種。

　　弓步：俗稱弓箭步。兩腿前後站立，兩腳相距本人腳長的 4～5 倍；前腿屈至大腿接近水平，腳尖微內扣不超過 5°；後腿伸膝挺直，腳掌內扣 45°。（圖 1）

　　馬步：俗稱騎馬步。兩腳開立，相距本人腳長的 3～3.5 倍，兩腳尖朝前；屈膝下蹲大腿接近水平，膝蓋與兩腳尖上下成一條線。（圖 2）

　　仆步：俗稱單叉，一腿屈膝全蹲，大腿貼緊小腿，膝微外展，另一腿直伸平仆接近地面，腳掌扣緊與小腿成 90°夾角。（圖 3）

　　虛步：又稱寒雞步。兩腳前後站立，前後相距本人腳長的 2 倍；重心移至後腿，後腿屈膝下蹲至大腿接近水平，腳掌外擺 45°；前腿腳尖點地，兩膝相距 10 公分。（圖 4）

　　歇步：兩腿左右交叉，靠近全蹲；前腳全腳掌著地，腳尖外展，後腳腳前掌著地，臀部微坐於後腿小腿上。（圖 5）

　　坐盤步：在歇步的形狀下，坐於地上，後腿的大小腿外側和腳背均著地。（圖 6）

　　丁步：兩腿併立，屈膝下蹲，大腿接近水平，一腳尖點地靠近另一腳內側腳窩處。（圖7）

　　併步：兩腿併立，屈膝下蹲，大腿接近水平。（圖8）

　　七星步：七星步是少林七星拳和大洪拳中獨有的步型。一腳內側腳窩內扣於另一腳腳尖，兩腿屈膝下蹲，接近水平。（圖9）

　　跪步：又稱小蹬山步。兩腳前後站立，相距本人腳長的 2.5 倍，前腿屈膝下蹲，後腿下跪，接近地面，後腳腳跟離地。（圖10）

　　高虛步：又稱高點步。兩腳前後站立，重心後移，後腿腳尖外擺 45°，前腿腳尖點地，兩腳尖相距一腳距離。（圖11）

　　翹腳步：在七星螳螂拳中又稱七星步，兩腿前後站立，相距本人腳長的 1.5 倍，後腳尖外擺 45°，屈膝下蹲，前腿直伸，腳跟著地，腳尖微內扣。（圖12）

基本手型

少林武術中常見的手型有拳、掌、鈎 3 種。

拳：

分為平拳和透心拳。

平拳：平拳是武術中較普遍的一種拳型，又稱方拳。四指屈向手心握緊，拇指橫屈扣緊食指。（圖

13）

　　透心拳：此拳主要用於打擊心窩處，故名。四指併攏捲握，中指突出拳面，拇指扣緊抵壓中指梢節處。（圖 14）

　　掌：

　　分為柳葉掌、八字掌、虎爪掌、鷹爪掌、鉗指掌。

　　柳葉掌：四指併立，拇指內扣。（圖 15）

　　八字掌：四指併立，拇指張開。（圖 16）

　　虎爪掌：五指分開，彎曲如鉤，形同虎爪。（圖 17）

　　鷹爪掌：又稱鎖喉手，拇指內扣，小指和無名指彎曲扣於掌心處，食指和中指分開內扣。（圖 18）

　　鉗指掌：五指分開，掌心內含。（圖 19）

　　鉤：

　　分為鉤手和螳螂鉤。

　　鉤手：屈腕，五指自然內合，指尖相攏。此鉤使用較廣，武術中提到的鉤均為此鉤。（圖 20）

　　螳螂鉤：又稱螳螂爪，屈腕成腕部上凸，無名指、小指屈指內握，食指、中指內扣，拇指梢端按貼於食指中節。（圖 21）

Basic stances

Usual stances in Shaolin Wushu are: bow stance, horse stance, crouch stance, empty stance, rest stance, cross – legged sitting, T – stance, feet – together stance, seven – star stance, kneel stance, high empty stance, and toes – raising stance, these twelve kinds.

Bow stance: commonly named bow – and – arrow stance. Two feet stand in tandem, the distance between two feet is about four or five times of length of one's foot; the front leg bends to the extent of the thigh nearly horizontal with toes slightly turned inward by less than 5°; the back leg stretches straight with the sole turned inward by 45°. (Figure 1)

Horse stance: commonly named riding step. two feet stand apart, the distance between two feet is 3~3.5 times of length of one's foot, with tiptoes turned forward; bend knees to squat downward, with thighs nearly horizontal, knees and two tiptoes in line. (Figure 2)

Crouch stance: commonly named single split. Bend the knee of one leg and squat entirely with thigh very close to lower leg and knee outspread slightly; straighten the other leg and crouch horizontally close to floor, keep the sole turned inward and forming an included angle of 90° with lower leg. (Figure 3)

Empty stance: also named cold – chicken stance. Two feet stand in tandem, the distance between two feet is 2 times of

length of one´s foot; transfer the barycenter to back leg, bend the knee of the back leg and squat downward to the extent of the thigh nearly horizontal, with the sole turned outward by 45°; keep the tiptoe of front leg on the ground, with distance between two knees of 10cm. (Figure 4)

Rest stance: cross the two legs at left and right, keep them close and entirely squat; keep the whole sole of the front foot on the ground with tiptoes turned outward, the front sole of the back foot on the ground, and buttocks slightly seated on the lower leg of the back leg. (Figure 5)

Cross – legged sitting: in the posture of rest stance, sit on the ground, with the outer sides of the thigh and lower leg of the back leg and instep on the ground. (Figure 6)

T – stance: two legs stand with feet together, bend knees and squat to the extent of the thighs nearly horizontal, with one tiptoe on the ground and close to inner side of the fossa of the other foot. (Figure 7)

Feet – together stance: two legs stand with feet together, bend knees and squat to the extent of the thigh nearly horizontal. (Figure 8)

Seven – star stance: Seven – star step is a unique step form in Shaolin Seven – star Boxing and Major Flood Boxing. Keep the inner side of the fossa of one foot turned inward onto tiptoe of the other foot, bend two knees and squat nearly horizontal. (Figure 9)

Kneel stance: also named small mountaineering stance. Two feet stand in tandem, the distance between two feet is 2.5

times of length of one´s foot, bend knee of the front leg and squat, kneel the back leg close to the floor, with the heel of back foot off the floor. (Figure 10)

High empty stance: also named high point stance. Two feet stand in tandem. Transfer the barycenter backward, turn the tiptoe of the back leg outward by 45°, with tiptoe of front leg on the ground, and the distance between two tiptoes is length of one foot. (Figure 11)

Toes −raising stance: also named seven −star stance in Seven−star Mantis Boxing. Two legs stand in tandem, and the distance between two legs is 1.5 times of length of one´s foot. Keep the tiptoe of back leg turned outward by 45°, bend knees and squat, straighten the front leg with heel on the ground and tiptoe turned inward slightly. (Figure 12)

Basic hand forms

Usual hand forms in Shaolin Wushu are: fist, palm and hook, these three kinds.

Fist: classified into straight fist and heart−penetrating fist.

Flat fist: a rather common fist form in Wushu, also named square fist. Hold the four fingers tightly toward the palm, and horizontally bend the thumb to button up the fore finger. (Figure 13)

Heart−penetrating fist: mainly used for striking the heart part. Put four fingers together and coil−hold them, the middle finger thrusts out the striking surface of the fist, the thumb

buttons up and presses the end and joint of the middle finger. (Figure 14)

Palm: classified into willow leaf palm, splay palm, tiger's claw palm, eagle's claw palm, fingers clamping palm.

Willow leaf palm: palm with four fingers up and thumb turned inward. (Figure 15)

Eight – shape palm: palm with four fingers up and thumb splay. (Figure 16)

Tiger's claw palm: palm with five fingers apart, bent as hook and like tiger's claw. (Figure 17)

Eagle's claw palm: also named throat locking hand, with the thumb turned inward, the little finger and middle finger turned onto palm, fore finger and middle finger apart and turned inward. (Figure 18)

Fingers clamp palm: palm with five fingers apart and palm drawn in. (Figure 19)

Hook: classified into hook hand and mantis hook.

Hook hand: bend the wrist, five fingers drawn in naturally with fingertips together. This hook is used in wide range, the hook mentioned in Wushu refers to this. (Figure 20)

Mantis hook: also named mantis' claw, bend wrist into wrist bulge upward, the ring finger and little finger bend to hold inward, with fore finger and fore middle finger turned inward and end of thumb pressed on the middle joint of the fore finger. (Figure 21)

白猿獻書套路簡介
Brief Introduction to the White Ape Offering Book

白猿獻書套路簡介

　　七星螳螂拳是清初拳師王郎在研究螳螂捕蟬時運用兩臂劈、砍、刁、閃的捕鬥技巧而創編的一種象形拳法。後王郎入少林寺 3 年，向寺僧傳授螳螂拳法。白猿獻書是七星螳螂拳其中的一個套路，該套路剛柔並濟、長短互用、手到腳到、貫穿緊湊、節奏明快、勁整力圓、周身相合、勾摟纏封、變化無窮。

　　Seven－star mantis boxing is a kind of shape－simulating boxing, which was developed and compiled by Wang Lang, a boxer at early Qing Dynasty, applying the capturing and fighting skills of the two arms when he researched the scene of mantis capturing cicada. Later, Wang Lang stayed at Shaolin Temple for 3 years, and taught mantis boxing to the monks of this temple. White Ape Offering Book is one of the routines in seven－star mantis boxing, which uses the temper force with grace, both long and short actions, harmonious and consistent actions of the hands and feet, forthright rhythm, integral strength and complete force, the actions of hook, grad, twining and closing, being coherent, compact and most changeful.

白猿獻書套路動作名稱
Action Names of Routine White Ape Offering Book

第一段　Section One

1. 預備勢
   Preparatory posture
2. 挑戳雙封手
   Uppercut, parry and close – up hands
3. 推掌沖拳
   Push palm and thrust fist
4. 甩梁
   Swing girder
5. 疊肘
   Fold elbow
6. 左封右崩捶
   Left wrap and right snap hammar
7. 採三手玉環步
   Grab hand three times in Jade – ring step

白猿獻書套路動作名稱

第二段　Section Two

8. 轉身底叫

Turn body and call in low position

9. 上下叫連環戳

High and low call with interlink jab

10. 左封右崩捶

Left wrap and right snap hammer

11. 採三手玉環步

Grasp hand three times in Jade−ring step

12. 左封右崩捶

Left wrap and right snap hammar

第三段　Section Three

13. 轉身左右雙幫肘

Turn body and help both elbows

14. 圈捶

Circular hammer

15. 採三手玉環步

Grab hand three times in Jade−ring step

16. 左封右崩捶

Left wrap and right snap hammer

17. 轉身左右鉤子步

Turn body with left and right hook step

18. 上步雙鉤

Step forward with double hooks

19. 抹眉千眼

Smear eyebrow and jab eyes

20. 下勢秘肘

Secret elbow in down posture

21. 左封右秘肘

Left wrap and right secret elbow

22. 左採右秘肘

Left pick and the right secret elbow

23. 左封右秘肘

Left wrap and right secret elbow

24. 轉身雙封手

Turn body and close-up hands

25. 收　勢

Closing form

圖 1

白猿獻書套路動作圖解

Action Illustrations of Routine white Ape Offering Book

第一段　Section One

1. 預備勢　Preparatory posture

(1) 兩腳自然站立，兩手下垂成立正姿勢；目視前方。（圖 1）

(1) Stand at attention with feet together and two hands hung naturally. Eyes look forward.〔Figure 1〕

圖2

（2）上動不停。雙手向兩側緩緩舉起，手心翻轉向上，再向裏收翻轉成手心向下，手與肩平；目視前方。（圖2、圖2附圖）

圖 2 附圖

(2) Keep the above action, two hands raise up to both sides slowly, turn over the palm up. then draw the palm inward and turn it over, with the palm down at the shoulder height. Eyes look forward. (Figure 2, Attached figure 2)

圖 3

(3) 上動不停。兩掌下按於腹前，掌指相對；目視前方。（圖 3、圖 3 附圖）

要點：挺胸塌腰，頭正頸直；雙手翻轉與下按要連貫一致。

白猿獻書套路動作圖解

圖 3 附圖

(3) Keep the above action, with palm down, press two palms before the abdomen with the palm down and the fingers of two palms opposite. Eyes look forward.（Figure 3, Attached figure 3）

Key points: keep chest out and abdomen in, head being correctitude and neck straight; two hands turn over and press shall be coherent and consistent.

圖4

2. 挑戳雙封手
Uppercut, parry and close-up hands

　（1）接上勢。左腳向前上一步，左手向前自然擺
動；右手變拳微向後擺；目視前下方。（圖4）

　（1）Follow the above posture, the left foot takes a step
forward, the left hand swings forward naturally, change the
right hand into fist to slightly swing backward. Eyes look
forward down.〔Figure 4〕

白猿獻書套路動作圖解

圖 5

(2)上動不停。右拳直臂上挑；左手迎擊右前臂內
側；目視右拳。（圖 5）

(2) Keep the above action, stretch the right arm straight
to raise the right fist, the left hand counterpunches the inner
side of the right forearm. Eyes look at the right fist.
〔Figure 5〕

圖6

（3）上動不停。右臂繼續上挑，屈肘回收於右耳處；左手向前伸出；目視前方。（圖6）

(3) Keep the above action, the right arm continuously uppercuts up, bend the arm and draw it back toward the right ear, the left hand stretches forward. Eyes look forward.〔Figure 6〕

白猿獻書套路動作圖解

圖 7

(4)上動不停。右腳上前跨步，右拳向前沖出，與左掌迎擊；左腿彎曲，身體下坐成七星步；目視前方。（圖 7）

(4) Keep the above action, the right foot strides forward, the right fist thrusts forward and counterpunches the left palm; bend the left leg, the body squats into the seven-star stance. Eyes look forward. 〔Figure 7〕

圖 8

(5) 上動不停。重心後移；右腿向後撤一步，雙手在身前交叉，右手在外，左手在內；目視雙手。（圖8）

(5) Keep the above action, move the barycenter back, the right leg takes a step back, cross two hands before the body, with the right hand outward, the left one inward. Eyes look at two hands. ﹝ Figure 8 ﹞

白猿獻書套路動作圖解

圖 9

(6) 上動不停。雙臂在胸前絞動，向右翻轉，兩掌根相對；目視雙手。（圖 9）

(6) Keep the above action, two arms twist and swing in front of the chest, turn over rightward, with the bases of two palms opposite. Eyes look at the two hands.（Figure 9）

圖 10

（7）上動不停。右掌向前探出，左手收於右胸前；
目視右手。（圖 10）

(7) Keep the above action, the right palm stretches
forward, draw back the left hand before the chest. Eyes
look at the right hand.（Figure 10）

圖 11

(8)上動不停。右掌回收變鉤於胸前；左手向前探出，高與肩平。（圖11）

(8) Keep the above action, draw back the palm and change it into hook hand in front of the chest, the left hand stretches forward at the shoulder height.（Figure 11）

圖 12

(9)上動不停。左手回收成鉤，重心後移，身體後坐，左腳收成虛步；目平視前方。（圖 12）

(9) Keep the above action, draw back the left hand and change it into hook hand, shift the barycenter back, draw back the left foot and change into the empty stance. Eyes look forward horizontally.〔Figure 12〕

圖 13

3. 推掌沖拳
Push palm and thrust fist

(1)接上勢。起身，上左腳成左弓步；雙手回收，右手變拳抱於腰間，左手變掌向前推出，成弓步推掌；目視前方。（圖13）

(1) Follow the above posture, the body stands up, the left foot steps forward and change into the left bow stance; draw back two hands, change the right hand into fist and hold it on the waist, change the left hand into palm and push it forward and change to push palm in bow stance. Eyes look forward.〔Figure 13〕

圖 14

（2）上動不停。繼續上右步，成右弓步；右拳從腰際向前推出，與左掌相擊，左掌護於右臂內側成弓步沖拳，拳心向下；目視前方。（圖 14）

（2）Keep the above action, the right foot continuously steps forward and change into the right bow stance. The right fist thrusts forward from the waist and beats with the left palm. the left palm guards inner side of the right arm with the fist-palm down. Eyes look forward.（Figure 14）

圖 15

4. 甩梁　Swing girder

接上勢。重心後移，左腳回收跳步，右腿屈膝上提，重心移於左腿；同時，左拳變掌在右臂上向下抓握成拳；右拳從懷裏抽出，向外屈肘崩擊，拳心向內；目視右拳。（圖 15、圖 15 附圖）

七星螳螂拳白猿獻書

圖 15 附圖

Follow the above posture, shift the barycenter back, draw back the left foot and jump, bend the right knee to lift the right foot and shift the barycenter to the left leg. At the same time, change the left fist into palm, then clench it into fist downward on the right arm, draw out the right fist from the bosom, bend and snap outward with the fist–palm inward. Eyes look at the right fist.（Figure 15, Attached figure 15）

圖 16

5. 疊肘　Fold elbow

(1)接上勢。落右腳，左手在右臂外側向前推出，手心向前，手指向上；右拳回抱腰間；目視前方。（圖 16）

(1) Follow the above posture, the right foot lands, the left hand pushes forward at the outer side of the right arm with the palm forward and the fingers up; draw back the right fist and hold it on the waist. Eyes look forward. 〔Figure 16〕

圖17

(2)上動不停。身體下蹲成馬步，右臂屈肘，向下疊肘於體前，左掌裏抱迎擊右肘；目視右肘。（圖17、圖17附圖）

白
猿
獻
書
套
路
動
作
圖
解

圖 17 附圖

(2) Keep the above action, squat the body down to make the horse stance, fold elbow downward in front of the body with the right elbow bent, hold the left palm inward and counterpunch the right elbow. Eyes look at the right elbow.（Figure 17, Attached figure 17）

圖 18

6. 左封右崩捶
Left wrap and right snap hammar

（1）接上勢。身體右轉 90°，上右腳，向前滑步；左手向下橫抓，右拳收回胸前；目平視前方。（圖18）

(1) Follow the above posture, step the right foot forward and turn the body 90° to the right to make a sliding step; the left hand grab downward horizontally, draw back the right fist and hold it on the waist. Eyes look forward horizontally.（Figure 18）

白猿獻書套路動作圖解

圖 19

(2)上動不停。右拳從懷裏向前崩出，再屈肘回收；左腿屈膝成蹬山步，左手附在右肘下；目視右拳。（圖 19）

(2) Keep the above action, the right fist snap forward from the bosom, then bend elbow and draw it back with the left hand putting under the right elbow; bend knee of the left leg and form the mountaineering step. Eyes look at the right fist.（Figure 19）

七星螳螂拳白猿獻書

圖 20

7. 採三手玉環步
Grasp hand three times in Jade-ring step

(1) 接上勢。起身，右手向外採抓變拳；目視右拳。（圖 20）

(1) Follow the above posture, the body stands up, the right hand grabs outward into fist. Eyes look at the right fist. [Figure 20]

白
猿
獻
書
套
路
動
作
圖
解

圖 21

(2) 上動不停。右手變拳後回抱腰間，左手向前採
手變拳；目視左拳。（圖 21）

(2) Keep the above action, change the right hand into
fist and hold it on the waist, the left hand grabs forward
into fist. Eyes look at the left fist.〔Figure 21〕

圖 22

（3）上動不停。右拳從腰際經左拳上方向前上方沖出，拳心向上；身體直立，重心移於右腿；目視前方。（圖 22）

（3）Keep the above action, the right fist thrusts forward through above the left fist from the waist, with the fist–palm up; the body stands up, shift the barycenter to the right leg. Eyes look forward.（Figure 22）

圖 23

(4) 上動不停。左手從右臂外側向前上方穿出，右拳同時回收腰間，身體向前傾斜，下肢動作不變；目視前方。（圖 23）

(4) Keep the above action, the left hand threads forward from outside of the right arm, at the same time, draw back the right fist on the waist, the body slants forward, keep the action of the lower limb unchangeable. Eyes look forward. (Figure 23)

圖 24

(5) 上動不停。左腳上一步，同時上右腳跟步；左手變拳回帶向左平擺，身體下蹲；右掌從腰際向左下方推擊；目視前方。（圖 24）

(5) Keep the above action, the left foot takes a step forward, at the same time, the right foot steps forward into the follow –up step. Change the left hand into fist for horizontal swing, the body squats down, the right palm pushes left downward from the waist. Eyes look forward. (Figure 24)

圖 25

第二段 Section Two

8. 轉身底叫
Turn body and call in low position

⑴接上勢。起身，雙手在胸前轉動，掌心向上；目視雙手。（圖 25）

(1) Follow the above posture, the body stands up, turn two hands in front of the chest with the palm up. Eyes look at two hands.（Figure 25）

圖 26

（2）上動不停。身體右轉 180°。同時，對手從胸前轉動，在頭上方變拳，然後從左上方向右下方畫弧收回，拳心相對；目視雙拳。（圖 26）

(2) Keep the above action, the bldy turns 180° to the right. At the same time, turn two hands in front of the chest and change into fist above the head, then draw curves from the left upward to right downward and draw back, with the fist–palm oposite. Eyes lock at two fists. (Figure 26)

白猿獻書套路動作圖解

圖 27

9. 上下叫連環戳
High and low call with interlink jab

（1）接上勢。右腳向前上步，左腳隨即跟步；重心上提，雙手向上托舉；目視前方。（圖27）

(1) Follow the above posture, the right foot steps forward and the left one follows up. Rise the barycenter and lift two hands upwad. Eyes look forward. ﹙Figure 27﹚

圖 28

(2)上動不停。兩腳先右後左再各上一步，雙手回拉於小腹前，身體後坐，重心後移；目視雙手。（圖28）

(2) Keep the above action, two feet step forward again with the right one first and then the left one, pull back two hands in front of the lower abdomen, shift the barycenter back. Eyes look at two hands. ﹝Figure 28﹞

圖 29

(3)上動不停。右腳向前上步，隨即左腳跟步；雙手向上托舉。（圖 29）

(3) Keep the above action, the right foot steps forward, then the left one follows up; two hands lift upward. （Figure 29）

圖 30

⑷上動不停。雙手由上向回拉，身體後坐，重心後移，左腿微屈；目視雙手。（圖 30）

⑷ Keep the above action, pull back two hands upward, shift the barycenter back. Bend the left leg slightly. Eyes look at two hands.（Figure 30）

圖 31

(5) 上動不停。右腳向前跨步，隨即左腳跟步；身體上提，雙手向上托舉；目視前方。（圖 31）

(5) Keep the above action, the right foot strides forward, then the left one follows up. The body lifts and two hands rise upward. Eyes look forward.（Figure 31）

七星螳螂拳白猿獻書

圖 32

（6）上動不停。雙手由上向下回拉，身體後坐，重心後移，左腿微屈；目視雙手。（圖 32）

(6) Keep the above action, draw back two hands from up to down. The body pulls backward, shift the barycenter back, bend the left leg slightly. Eyes look at two hands. (Figure 32)

圖 33

(7) 上動不停。以上動作在做完三遍後，左拳回收
於腰間，右拳向前屈肘圈插，拳心向下，拳眼向後，
高與肩平；目平視右拳。（圖 33）

(7) Keep the above action, draw back the left fist on
the waist after doing the above actions three times, bend
the right elbow and the right fist closes up and inserttes
forward, with the fist – palm down, the fist – hole backward
at the shoulder height. Eyes look at the right fist. 〔Figure
33〕

圖 34

(8) 上動不停。左拳在右臂外抄拳；目視左手。
（圖 34）

(8) Keep the above action, uppercut with the left to the outer side of the right arm. Eyes look at the left hand. （Figure 34）

圖 35

(9) 上動不停。左腳上步，右腳跟步成蹬山步；左臂屈肘向外格擋；右拳向前沖出，拳心向下，高與肩平；目視前方。（圖 35）。

(9) Keep the above action, the left foot steps forward and the right one follows up to make the mountaineering step, the left arm parries outward with the elbow bent, the right one thrusts forward with the fist−palm down at the shoulder height. Eyes look forward. 〔 Figure 35 〕

圖 36

10. 左封右崩捶
Left wrap and right snap hammer

（1）接上勢。起身，向前上右步，跟左腳；右拳收
於腰際，左手向下橫抓變拳，拳心向下；目視前方。
（圖 36）

（1）Follow the above posture, the body stands up, the
right foot steps forward and the left one follows up, draw
back the right fist on the waist, the left hand grabs
downward horizontally into fist, with fist-palm down.
Eyes look forward.（Figure 36）

圖 37

(2) 上動不停。右拳經左拳上向斜上方崩出，拳心
向內，成蹬山步；目視右拳。（圖 37）

要點：崩拳迅猛有力，收回要有反彈力，上下動
作要連貫一致。

(2) Keep the above action, the right fist snaps forward
aslant ahead through the left fist, with the fist –palm
inward, forming the mountaineering step. Eyes look at the
right fist.（Figure 37）

Key points: snap punch shall be swift and powerful,
the drawing back shall exert rebounding force, all the
actions shall be coherent and consistent.

圖 38

11. 採三手玉環步
Grasp hand three times in Jade-ring step

（1）接上勢。右手向下採抓，目視右手（圖 38）

（1）Follow the above posture, the body stands up, the right hand grabs downward. Eyes look at the right hand. （Figure 38）

圖 39

(2)上動不停。右手採抓後稍往懷裡收回，同時左
手伸出向下採抓；目視左手。（圖 39）

(2) Keep the above action, the right hand draws inward
slightly after grabbing, the left hand stretches out and grabs
downward. Eyes look at the left hand.〔Figure 39〕

圖 40

(3) 上動不停。右拳從腰際向胸前上方沖出，拳心
向上；上體左轉；目視前方。（圖 40）

(3) Keep the above action, the right fist rushes upward
from the waist before the chest with the fist –palm up;
Upper body turns to the left. Eyes look forward.〔 Figure
40 〕

白
猿
獻
書
套
路
動
作
圖
解

圖 41

(4) 上動不停。右轉身，左手經右臂外側向前穿出；同時，左腳腳跟抬起，身體前傾，重心前移；目視左手。（圖 41）

(4) Keep the above action, the body turns to right, the left hand threads forward through the outer side of the right arm. At the same time, the left heel uplifts, the body leans forward, shift the barycenter forward. Eyes look at the left hand. ﹝Figure 41﹞

七星螳螂拳白猿獻書

圖 42

(5)上動不停。左腳向前上一步，右腿成外擺下跪
式，左腿屈膝支撐；左手採抓變拳，向左、向外回
拉，右掌從腰際向前、向左推出，掌心向左，掌指向
前；目視左前下方。（圖 42）

(5) Keep the above action, the left foot strides a step
forward, the right leg show the posture of kneeling down
with outward swing, bend knee of the left leg to support,
the left hand grabs and changes into fist, pull back leftward
and outward, the right palm pushes forward and leftward
through the waist with the palm leftward and the fingers
forward. Eyes look at the left ahead down.（Figure 42）

圖 43

12. 左封右崩捶
Left wrap and right snap hammar

(1) 接上勢。起身，右腳上步，左腳跟半步；右掌變拳回收於腰際，左手屈臂向下採封變拳；目視前下方。（圖 43）

(1) Follow the above posture, the body stands up, the right foot steps forward, the left one follows half a step; change the right palm into fist and draw back on the waist, bend the left arm and the left hand picks and grabs downward to change into fist. Eyes look ahead down. (Figure 43)

圖 44

　　(2) 上動不停。右拳經過胸前在左腕上向前上方崩擊，高與頜平，目視前方。（圖 44）

　　要點：採手變拳要靈活敏捷，崩拳要抖肩發力，有反彈力。

　　(2) Keep the above action, the right fist snaps forward above the left wrist through the front of the chest at the chin height. Eyes look forward.（Figure 44）

　　Key points: grabbing hand into fist shall be flexible and quick, snap punch shall make the shoulders snap to send the strength and have rebounding force.

白
猿
獻
書
套
路
動
作
圖
解

圖 45

第三段　Section Three

13. 轉身左右雙幫肘
Turn body and help both elbows

(1) 接上勢。身體左轉 90°，重心後移；雙手變掌上托；目視左下方。（圖 45）

(1) Follow the above posture, the body turns 90° to the left, shift the barycenter back; change two hands into palms and uplift. Eyes look down.〔Figure 45〕

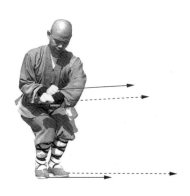

圖 46

(2) 上動不停。雙掌由左向裡回捋變拳；收右腳震腳併步，雙腿略屈膝，身體後坐；目視雙拳。（圖 46）

(2) Keep the above action, two palms grab back from left to inward and change into fists; draw back the right foot, stamp it and bring feet together, bend knees of two legs slightly. Eyes look at the two fists.（Figure 46）

圖 47

(3) 上動不停。左腳向左跨一步，跟右腳；右拳附於左臂內側向前推擊，左臂屈肘；同時，左轉身 90°；目視前方。（圖 47）

(3) Keep the above action, the left foot strides forward and the right one follows up; bend elbow of the left arm and push forward with the right fist attaching to the inner side of the left arm. At the same time, the body turns 90° to the left. Eyes look forward.（Figure 47）

圖 48

（4）上動不停。身體上提，再左轉身 90°，雙手在
胸前轉動變掌上托；目視雙手。（圖 48）

（4）Keep the above action, the body lifts and turns 90°
to the left, turn two hands in front of the chest and change
into fists to uplft. Eyes look at two hands.（Figure 48）

圖 49

(5)上動不停。雙掌在胸前後捋變拳；目視右前下方。（圖 49、圖 49 附圖）

圖 49 附圖

(5) Keep the above action, two palms grab in front of the chest and change into fists. Eyes look right ahead down. （Figure 49, Attached figure 49）

圖 50

(6)上動不停。右腳向前上跨一步，左腳跟步成蹬山步；左拳附於右臂內側向前推擊；目視前方。（圖50）

(6) Keep the above action, the right foot strides a step forward, the left one follows up to make the mountaineering step, the left fist attaches to the inner side of the right arm and pushes forward. Eyes look forward. 〔Figure 50〕

七星螳螂拳白猿獻書

圖 51

（7）上動不停。起身，同時稍右轉，雙掌上托；目
視雙手。（圖51）

（7）Keep the above action, the body stands up and at
the same time turns to the right slightly, two palms uplift.
Eyes look at two hands.（Figure 51）

圖 52

(8) 上動不停。身體右轉 90°成交叉步；雙掌回捋在胸前變拳。（圖 52）

(8) Keep the above action, the body turns 90° to the right into the cross stance. Grad two palms back and change them into fists before chest. 〔 Figure 52 〕

七星螳螂拳白猿獻書

圖 53

(9) 上動不停。上左步，跟右步，右拳附於左臂內側向前推擊；目視前方。（圖 53）

(9) Keep the above action, the left foot steps forward and the right one follows up, the right fist attaches to the inner side of the left arm and pushes forward. Eyes look forward.（Figure 53）

圖 54

(10) 上動不停。起身，同時左轉 90°，雙拳在胸前變掌上托；目視前下方。（圖 54）

(10) Keep the above action, the body stands up and at the same time turns 90° to the right, change two fists into palms before chest and uplift. Eyes look ahead down. (Figure 54)

圖 55

(11) 上動不停。雙掌回捋變拳；目視右前方。（圖 55）

(11) Keep the above action, two palms grab back into fists. Eyes look forward.〔Figure 55〕

圖 56

⑿ 上動不停。右腳向前上一步，左腳跟步成蹬山步；左拳附於右臂內側向前推擊；目平視前方。（圖56）

⑿ Keep the above action, the right foot steps forward, the left one follows up to make the mountaineering step, the left fist attaches to the inner side of the right arm and pushes forward. Eyes look forward horizontally. ﹝Figure 56﹞

圖 57

14. 圈捶　Circular hammer

接上勢。起身，右腳上步；右拳向前圈擊，左掌護於右腕內側，臂與肩平；目視前上方。（圖 57）

Follow the above posture, the body stands up, the right foot steps forward. The right fist strikes forward circularly and left one guards at inner side of the right wrist, keep the arm high with the shoulder height. Eyes look forward. (Figure 57)

圖 58

15. 採三手玉環步
Grab hand three times in jade-ring step

(1) 接上勢。起身，右手向外採抓變拳；目平視前
方。（圖 58）

(1) Follow the above posture, the body stands up, the
right hand grabs outward to change into fist. Eyes look
forward horizontally.（Figure 58）

圖 59

　　(2) 上動不停。身體略微右轉；同時，右拳收抱於腰間，拳心向上；左拳變掌，從胸前向前封抓變拳，拳心向下，拳面向右，高與肩平；目視左拳。（圖59）

　　(2) Keep the above action, the body turns to the right slightly. At the same time, draw back the right fist and hold it on the waist with the fist－palm up; change the left fist into palm, grab forward from the front of the chest and change into fist, with the fist－palm down and the fist－plane rightward at the shoulder height. Eyes look at the left fist. (Figure 59)

圖60

(3)上動不停。身體略向左轉；同時，右拳經左前
臂內側向前上方沖出，拳心斜向上，高與眼平；左拳
回收於右胸前，拳心向下；目視右拳。（圖60）

(3) Keep the above action, the body turns to the left
slightly. At the same time, the right palm thrusts ahead up
through the inner side of the left forearm with the fist –
palm up aslant at the eye height; draw back the left fist in
front of the chest with the fist–palm down. Eyes look at the
right fist.（Figure 60）

圖 61

（4）上動不停。身體向右擰轉 90°；右拳收回抱於腰間，拳心向上；左拳變掌，經右臂外側向前穿掌，掌心斜向上，掌指向左前方；目視左掌。（圖 61）

（4）Keep the above action, the body turns 90° to the right, draw back the right fist and hold it on the waist, with the fist-palm up; change the left fist into palm and thread forward through the outer side of the right arm, with the fist-palm up aslant, the fingers left forward. Eyes look at the left palm.（Figure 61）

圖 62

（5）上動不停。左腳向前跨一步，隨即右腳跟步；身體向左擰轉 90°，身體下蹲成玉環步；同時，左掌翻腕變拳向左側拉帶，拳心向下，高與肩平；右拳變掌，經胸前向左下方推出，置於左膝外側，掌心向左，掌指向前；目視左前方。（圖 62）

(5) Keep the above action, the left foot strides forward, then the right one follows up, the body turns 90° to the left, and squat into the jade-ring step. At the same time, turn over the wrist of the left palm into fist and pull leftward, with the fist-palm down at the shoulder height; change the right fist into palm to push downward through the front of the chest and put it on the outer side of the left knee, with the palm leftward, the fingers forward. Eyes look forward. （Figure 62）

圖 63

16. 左封右崩捶
Left wrap and right snap hammer

（1）接上勢。右腳向前上一步，左腳跟步；右手回收變拳；左手向下橫抓變拳。（圖 63）

(1) Follow the above posture, the body lifts up, the right foot steps forward and the left one follows up; draw back the right hand into fist, the left hand grabs downward horizontally and changes into fist.（Figure 63）

白猿獻書套路動作圖解

圖 64

(2) 上動不停。右拳經胸前、左臂向前上方崩擊；
目視前方。（圖 64）

(2) Keep the above action, the right fist snaps ahead
forward through the front of the chest and the left arm.
Eyes look forward.〔Figure 64〕

圖 65

17. 轉身左右鉤子步
Tun body with left and right hook step

（1）接上勢。起身，身體左轉 180°；雙手胸前交叉；目視雙手。（圖 65）

（1）Follow the above posture, the body stands up and tums 180° to the left. Two hands cross in front of the chest. Eyes look at two hands.（Figure 65）

圖 66

(2) 上動不停。上右步震腳併步；雙手翻轉，掌心相對。（圖 66、圖 66 附圖）

圖 66 附圖

(2) Keep the above action, the right foot steps forward, stamp it and bring the feet together, turn two hands over with the palms opposite. (Figure 66, Attached figure 66)

白
猿
獻
書
套
路
動
作
圖
解

圖 67

（3）上動不停。上左步成鉤子步，重心移於右腿，身體後坐；左手向外平抓成鉤，左臂與肩平；右掌成鉤，鉤尖向裡；目視前方。（圖 67）

(3) Keep the above action, the right foot steps forward into the hook step, move the barycenter to the right leg, the left hand grabs outward horizontally into hook, keep the right arm high with the shoulder; change the right palm into hook, with the hook-tip inward. Eyes look forward.（Figure 67）

七星螳螂拳白猿獻書

圖 68

(4)上動不停。動心前移，落左腳，身體左轉；左手向外摟抓；目視前方。（圖 68）

(4) Keep the above action, move the barycenter forward and the left foot lands, the body turns to the left, the left hand grabs forward. Eyes look forward.〔Figure 68〕

圖 69

(5)上動不停。左手回收；右手成掌，右臂屈臂置
於左臂上方；目平視前方。（圖 69）

(5) Keep the above action, draw back the left hand,
change the right hand into palm, bend the right arm to put it
above the left arm. Eyes lock forward horizontally.
（Figure 69）

圖 70

（6）上動不停。右手再向外勾摟，使鉤手高與肩平；同時上右腳成鉤子步，身體後坐；目視前方。（圖70）

（6）Keep the above action, the right hand grabs outward again into the hook at the shoulder height, at the same time, the right foot steps forward into the hook step. Eyes look forward.（Figure 70）

圖 71

18. 上步雙鉤
Step forward with double hooks

（1）接上勢。右腳落地，左右鉤手回收胸前變掌；上左腳，雙掌向前探出，臂與肩平；目視前方。（圖71）

（1）Follow the above posture, the right foot falls to the ground, draw back the left and right hook hand in front of the chest into palm; the left foot steps forward, two palms stretch and grab forward, keep the arm at the shoulder height. Eyes look forward.（Figure 71）

圖 72

(2)上動不停。雙掌勾抓回收至胸前成鉤手，右鉤手屈臂在上，左鉤手屈臂在下；重心後移成馬步；目視左方。（圖 72、圖 72 附圖）

重點：勾抓回收要輕靈快捷。

白
猿
獻
書
套
路
動
作
圖
解

圖 72 附圖

(2) Keep the above action, two palms grab into the hook hands before drawing back in front of the chest, bend the arms with the right hook hand up, the left one down, shift the barycenter to make the horse stance. Eyes look leftward. (Figure 72, Attached figure 72)

Key points: grabbing like a hook and drawing back shall be rapid.

圖 73

19. 抹眉千眼　Smear eyebrow and jab eyes

（1）接上勢。右鉤手變拳回收於腰際；左手變掌橫擺胸前；身體擰腰微右轉；目視左手。（圖 73、圖 73 附圖）

圖 73 附圖

(1) Follow the above posture, change the right hook hand into fist and draw it back on the waist, change the left hand into palm to swing horizontally before the chest. Twist the waist, The body turns to the right slightly. Eyes look at the left hand. (Figure 73, Attached figure 73)

圖 74

（2）上動不停。身體左轉；左掌向左平掃；目視前方。（圖 74）

（2）Keep the above action the body turns to the left and the left palm sweeps leftward horizontally. Eyes look forward.〔Figure 74〕

圖 75

（3）上動不停。抬左腳小跳再落步，右手成剪子手向前戳擊，高與肩平；同時，右腳向前彈踢；目視前方。（圖 75）

(3) Keep the above action, the left foot lifts and takes little jumping step, then lands down, change the right hand into scissors hand and thrust forward at the shoulder height. At the same time, the right foot snaps kick forward. Eyes look forward.（Figure 75）

圖 76

⑷上動不停。右腳回收，提膝；目視前方。（圖76）

要點：彈踢要繃直腳面，力達腳尖；戳擊要迅猛有力。

⑷Keep the above action, draw back the right foot and lift up the knee. Eyes look forward.（Figure 76）

Key points: the snap kick shall stretch the instep tightly with the strength reaching tiptoe; thrust quickly and forcefully.

圖 77

20. 下勢秘肘　Secret elbow in down posture

(1) 接上勢。雙手變掌，在胸前合擊；下肢姿勢不變；目視雙掌。（圖 77）

(1) Follow the above posture, change two hands into palms and make a joint attack in front of the chest. Keep the posture of the lower limbs unchangeable. Eyes look at two palms.（Figure 77）

圖 78

(2)上動不停。向右落右腳成右弓步；右手由懷裏
向右下方打秘肘；身體前傾，重心前移；左鉤手屈臂
向上略提，高過頭頂；目視前方。（圖 78）

(2) Keep the above action, the right foot lands rightward
into the right bow stance, the right hand beats from bosom
toward right down secretly; the body leans forward, shift
the barycenter forward, bend the left arm and the left hook
hand lifts up over head slightly. Eyes look forward.
(Figure 78)

圖 79

21. 左封右秘肘
Left wrap and right secret elbow

（1）接上勢。右手向外勾摟；左手抱於腰際；目視前方。（圖 79）

（1）Follow the above posture, grab the right hand outward and hold the left one on the waist. Eyes look forward.〔Figure 79〕

圖80

（2）上動不停。右手收回腰際；左手向前勾摟；下
肢姿勢不變；目平視前方。（圖80）

（2）Keep the above action, draw back the right hand on
the waist and grab the left one forward. Keep the posture
of the lower limbs unchangeable. Eyes look forward
horizontally.（Figure 80）

白
猿
獻
書
套
路
動
作
圖
解

圖 81

(3)上動不停。右腳向前上一步，左腳跟步；左手
繼續向裏勾摟，右手從懷裏向前打秘肘；目視右手。
（圖 81）

(3) Keep the above action, the right foot steps forward
and the left one follows up, the left hand continues to grab
inward and the right one strikes forward from the bosom
with the secret elbow. Eyes look at the right hand.（Figure
81）

圖 82

22. 左採右秘肘
Left pick and the right secret elbow

(1)接上勢。上左腳，跟右腳；左手在右臂外側向前推洗；右手鉤手回收；目視前方。（圖82、圖82附圖）

白猿獻書套路動作圖解

圖 82 附圖

(1) Follow the above posture, the left foot steps forward and the right one follows up, the left hand pushes forward at the outer side of the right arm with the palmback rubbing the arm. Change the right hand into hook hand and draw it back. Eyes look forward.〔Figure 82, Attached figure 82〕

七星螳螂拳白猿獻書

圖83

　（2）上動不停。左手向外採抓成鉤手，擺架於頭部左側；右手向左前下方打祕肘；目視前下方。（圖83）

　（2）Keep the above action,the left hand grabs outward into the hook hand and parries on the left side of the head; the right hand strikes left ahead down with the secret elbow. Eyes look ahead down.（Figure 83）

圖 84

23. 左封右秘肘
Left wrap and right secret elbow

⑴接上勢。起身，上右步，跟左腳；右鉤手向外勾摟；左手勾收於腰際；目視前方。（圖 84）

⑴ Follow the above posture, the body stands up, the right foot steps forward and the left one follows up, the right hook hand grabs outward, draw back the left hook hand on the waist. Eyes look forward.（Figure 84）

圖 85

（2）上動不停。左鈎手向右、向裏勾摟；右手繼續勾摟收回腰際；下肢姿勢不變；目視左鈎手。（圖85）

（2）Keep the above action, the left hook hand grabs inward, the right hook hand continues to grab and draw back on the waist, keep the posture of the lower limbs unchangeable. Eyes look at the left hook hand.〔Figure 85〕

白
猿
獻
書
套
路
動
作
圖
解

圖 86

(3)上動不停。右手經腰際向前打秘肘；左鉤手回
收於胸前；目視前方。（圖 86）

(3) Keep the above action, the right hand strikes
forward with the secret elbow through the waist, draw back
the left hook hand in front of the chest. Eyes look forward.
（Figure 86）

七星螳螂拳白猿獻書

圖 87

24. 轉身雙封手

Turn body and close-up hands

(1)接上勢。起身,重心後移,同時左轉身180°;雙手在小腹前向上交叉;目視雙手。(圖 87、圖 87附圖)

圖 87 附圖

(1) Follow the above posture, the body stands up, shift the barycenter back. At the same time the body turns 180° to the left. Two hands cross upward in front of the lower abdomen. Eyes look at two hands. ﹝ Figure 87, Attached figure 87 ﹞

圖 88

(2) 上動不停。雙手從下向上在胸前交叉翻轉；下肢姿勢不變；目視雙手。（圖 88）

(2) Keep the above action, cross and turn over two hands from down to up in front of the chest. Keep the posture of the lower limbs unchangeable. Eyes look at two hands. (Figure 88)

白猿獻書套路動作圖解

圖 89

(3) 上動不停。右手向前探出；左手搭在右肩處；目視前方。（圖 89）

(3) Keep the above action, the right hand stretches forward and the left one shall be put on the shoulder. Eyes look forward.〔Figure 89〕

圖 90

⑷上動不停。右手回帶成鉤手；左手從右肘上側
向前探出，高與肩平；目視前方。（圖 90）

⑷ Keep the above action, the right hand pulls back
and changes into the hook hand, the left hand stretches
forward from the upper side of the right elbow at the
shoulder height. Eyes look forward.（Figure 90）

圖 91

(5)上動不停。左手回帶成鉤手，身體下蹲成封手式，左鉤手在外，右鉤手在內；目視左方。（圖 91）

(5) Keep the above action, the left hand pulls back and changes into the hook hand, the body squats down and close –up hands, with the left hook hand outside and the right one inside. Eyes look leftward.（Figure 91）

圖 92

25. 收勢　Closing form

（1）接上勢。起身，身體略右轉，雙手變掌，從裏向外、向上、向下畫弧摟抓，同時成馬步；目視右方。（圖 92）

（1）Follow the above posture, the body stands up and turns to the right slightly, change two hands into palms, draw a curve and grab outward, upward and downward from inside, at the same time, show the horse stance. Eyes look rightward.（Figure 92）

白猿獻書套路動作圖解

圖 93

(2) 上動不停。雙掌摟抓變拳回抱腰際，拳心向上，左腳上步併步；目視前方。（圖 93）

(2) Keep the above action, grab two palms into fists and hold them on the waist with the fist–palm up, the left foot steps forward and bring feet together. Eyes look forward.〔Figure 93〕

圖 94

(3)上動不停。雙手自然下垂，成立正式；目視前方。（圖 94）

要點：併步與抱拳要協調一致，挺胸收腹；平心靜氣，體態自然，精神內斂。

(3) Keep the above action, two hands hang naturally into standing up. Eyes look forward. 〔 Figure 94 〕

Key points: harmonize the action of bringing the feet together and holding the fist, lift the chest and draw the abdomen; calmly, posture is natural and vital energy colects inward.

全套動作示意圖

Demonstration of All the Actions

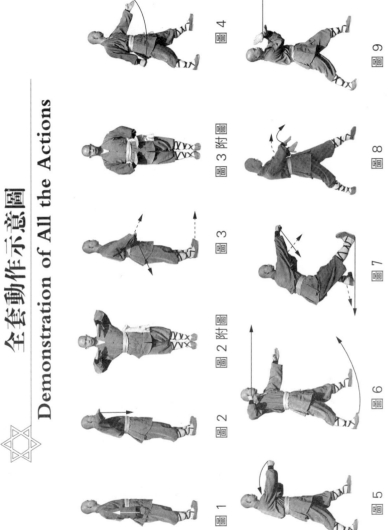

七星螳螂拳白猿獻書

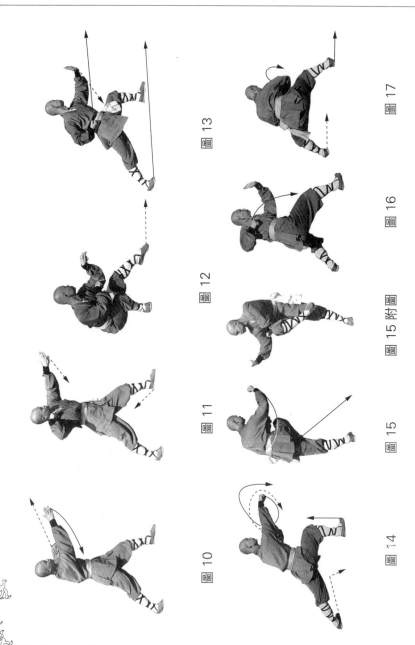

圖 17

圖 16

圖 15 附圖

圖 15

圖 14

圖 13

圖 12

圖 11

圖 10

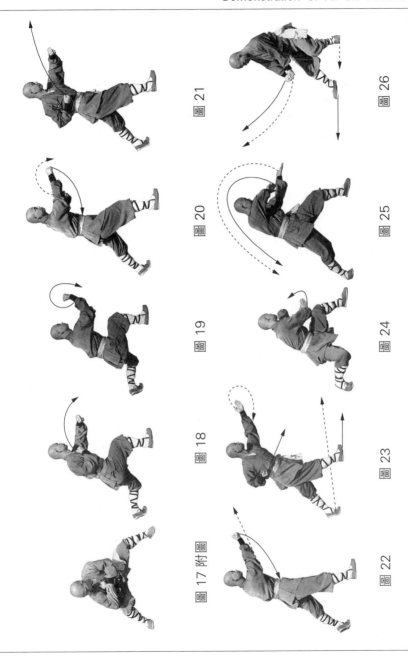

全套動作示意圖

圖 21

圖 20

圖 19

圖 18

圖 17 附圖

圖 26

圖 25

圖 24

圖 23

圖 22

七星螳螂拳白猿獻書

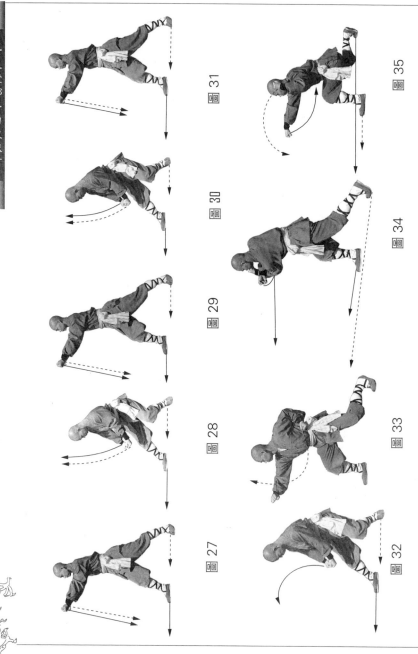

圖 31

圖 30

圖 29

圖 28

圖 27

圖 35

圖 34

圖 33

圖 32

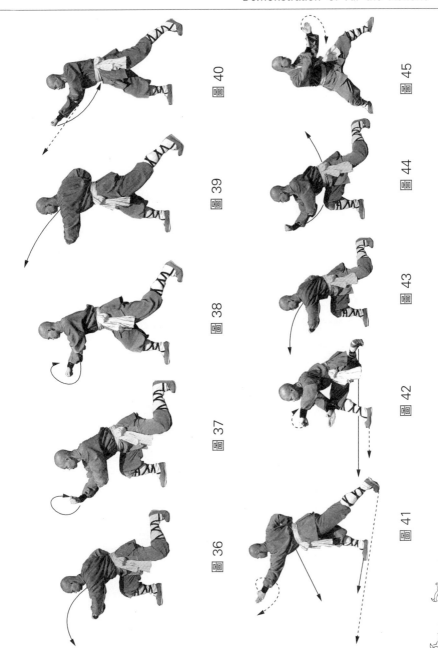

全套動作示意圖

圖 36　圖 37　圖 38　圖 39　圖 40

圖 41　圖 42　圖 43　圖 44　圖 45

七星螳螂拳白猿獻書

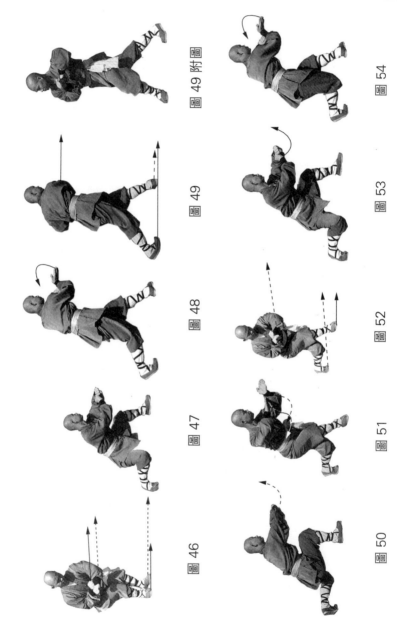

圖 49 附圖　圖 49　圖 48　圖 47　圖 46

圖 54　圖 53　圖 52　圖 51　圖 50

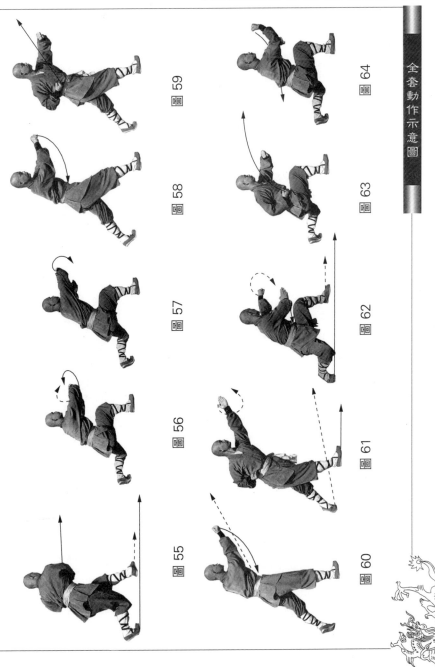

全套動作示意圖

圖 59

圖 58

圖 57

圖 56

圖 55

圖 64

圖 63

圖 62

圖 61

圖 60

七星螳螂拳白猿獻書

圖 68

圖 67

圖 66 附圖

圖 66

圖 65

圖 72 附圖

圖 72

圖 71

圖 70

圖 69

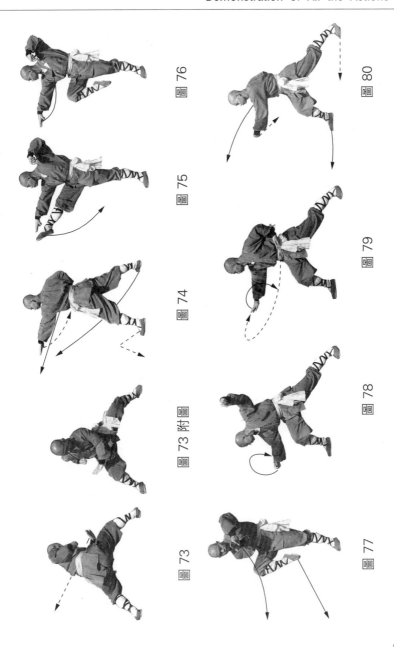

全套動作示意圖

圖 76

圖 75

圖 74

圖 73 附圖

圖 73

圖 80

圖 79

圖 78

圖 77

七星螳螂拳白猿獻書

圖 84

圖 88

圖 83

圖 87 附圖

圖 82 附圖

圖 87

圖 82

圖 86

圖 81

圖 85

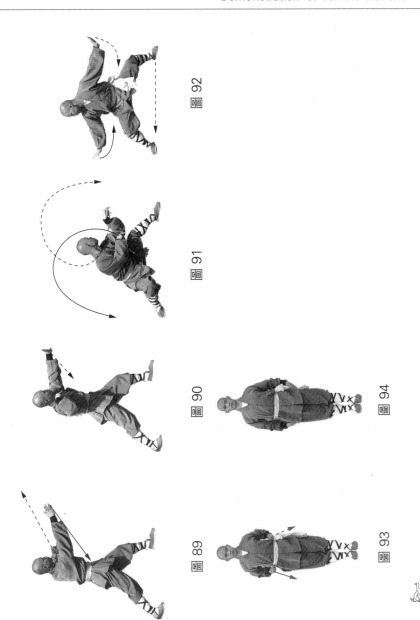

圖 92

圖 91

圖 90

圖 94

圖 89

圖 93

國家圖書館出版品預行編目資料

七星螳螂拳白猿獻書／耿　軍　著
——初版，——臺北市，大展，2006〔民95〕
面；21公分，——（少林傳統功夫漢英對照系列；1）
ISBN　978-957-468-496-0（平裝）
1.拳術—中國
528.97　　　　　　　　　　　　　　95016836

七星螳螂拳白猿獻書

ISBN－13：978-957-468-496-0
ISBN－10：957-468-496-2

著　　者／耿　軍
責任編輯／朱曉峰
發 行 人／蔡森明
出 版 者／大展出版社有限公司
社　　址／台北市北投區（石牌）致遠一路2段12巷1號
電　　話／（02）28236031・28236033・28233123
傳　　眞／（02）28272069
郵政劃撥／01669551
網　　址／www.dah-jaan.com.tw
E－mail／service@dah-jaan.com.tw
登 記 證／局版臺業字第2171號
承 印 者／高星印刷品行
裝　　訂／建鑫印刷裝訂有限公司
排 版 者／弘益電腦排版有限公司
授 權 者／北京人民體育出版社
初版1刷／2006年（民95年）11月

定　價／180元

推理文學經典巨著，中文版正式授權

名偵探明智小五郎與怪盜的挑戰與鬥智
名偵探柯南、金田一都讚嘆不已

日本推理小說鼻祖－江戶川亂步

1894年10月21日出生於日本三重縣名張〈現在的名張市〉。本名平井太郎。
就讀於早稻田大學時就曾經閱讀許多英、美的推理小說。
畢業之後曾經任職於貿易公司，也曾經擔任舊書商、新聞記者等各種工作。
1923年4月，在『新青年』中發表「二錢銅幣」。
筆名江戶川亂步是根據推理小說的始祖艾德嘉‧亞藍波而取的。
後來致力於創作許多推理小說。
1936年配合「少年俱樂部」的要求所寫的『怪盜二十面相』極受人歡迎，
陸續發表『少年偵探團』、『妖怪博士』共26集……等
適合少年、少女閱讀的作品。

1 ～ 3 集　定價300元　試閱特價189元